A TASTE OF NEWBERYS

FOR READERS AND EATERS

By Melissa Dalton Hunt

Enjoy the goodies
within!
Melissa Hunt

"The Newbery Medal and Newbery Honor books are named after John Newbery, the famous eighteenth century publisher and seller of children's books in England. They are awarded annually by the Association for Library Service to Children, a division of the American Library Association, to the author of the most distinguished contribution to American literature for children."

> "Some books should be tasted, some devoured, but only a few should be chewed and digested thoroughly." Francis Bacon

For a list of Newbery Medal and Honor Books search the Newbery Medal Home Page at the Association for Library Service to Children.

www.ala.org/alsc/awardsgrants/bookmedia/newberymedal/newberymedal
Whew!

INTRODUCTION

Reading as a family and eating meals together bring communication, love, and bonding into our homes. Enjoy reading these Newbery books aloud, then add flavor to the stories by preparing the recipes that go with them. While you're in the kitchen together, you can chat about these wonderful books, helping your family gain a taste for great literature.

Melissa Dalton Hunt

Text copyright © 2018 by Melissa Dalton Hunt

Published by A TASTE OF NEWBERYS

DEDICATED TO:

♥

my flashlight-under-the-covers-
reading grandkids who surround
me and astound me

♥

my husband who so willingly
taste tested every recipe

A TASTE OF NEWBERYS
NATIONAL FOOD DAYS

January 2	Day of Crepes in France	8
January 4	Spaghetti Day	10
January 22	Southern Food Day	6
February 4	Homemade Soup Day	38
February 6	Chopsticks Day	16
February 22	Cook a Sweet Potato Day	30
April 23	Picnic Day	22
April 30	Raisin Day	44
May 15	Chocolate Chip Cookies Day	20
June 5	Gingerbread Day	4
July 7	Macaroni Day	32
August 22	Eat a Peach Day	28
August 24	Waffle Day	36
September 21	International Banana Festival	2
October	Apple Month	34
October 10	Angel Food Cake Day	42
October 22	Nut Day	40
November 5	Donut Day	46
December 12	Cocoa Day	18
December 13	Beef Stew Day	24
December 17	Maple Syrup Day	14
December 28	Chocolate Candy Day	26
December 31	Dutch Donuts New Years Eve	12

TABLE OF CONTENTS

The Voyage of Dr. Dolittle 1
    Deep Fried Banana Bites with Honey 2

A Day on Skates 3
    Spicy Gingerbread 4

On the Banks of Plum Creek 5
    Ruby Louise Franklin Dalton's Corn Bread 6

Pancakes-Paris 7
    Dessert or Breakfast Crepes 8

The 21 Balloons 9
    Baked Zucchini Angel Hair 10

The Wheel on the School 11
    Oliebollen – Dutch Donut 12

Miracles on Maple Hill 13
    Home Made Maple Syrup 14

The Cricket in Times Square 15
    Chow Mein 16

A Wrinkle in Time 17
    Dark and Stormy Hot Chocolate 18

Frog and Toad Together 19
    Mimmie's Chocolate Chip Cookies 20

Abel's Island 21
    Abel's Island Picnic 22

Sarah Plain and Tall   23
    Sarah's Beef Stew   24

Maniac Magee   25
    Homemade Mars Bars   26

Holes   27
    Spiced Peaches   28

Bud, Not Buddy   29
    Festive Sweet Potato Pie   30
    Best Pie Crust

Because of Winn-Dixie   31
    Squiglly Easy Cheesey Mac   32

A Year Down Yonder   33
    Baked Apple Sundaes   34

Everything on a Waffle   35
    Cinnamon Roll Waffles   36

The Tale of Despereaux   37
    Clam Chowder   38

Princess Academy   39
    Honey Roasted Nuts   40

Moon Over Manifest   41
    Over the Moon Angel Food Cake   42

The One and Only Ivan   43
    Yogurt and White Chocolate Covered Raisins   44

Flora and Ulysses   45
    Spudnuts (Donuts)   46

THE VOYAGES OF DOCTOR DOLITTLE

Newbery Medal 1923, By Hugh Lofting

Reading Level Grades 4 – 7

Doctor Dolittle, the veterinarian who can actually talk to animals, sets sail on the high seas for new adventures with Polynesia the parrot, Jip the dog, Chee-Chee the monkey, and young Tommy Stubbins. Together they travel to Spidermonkey Island, brave a shipwreck, and meet the incredible Great Glass Sea Snail.

MY FAVORITE QUOTE

"Indeed, the vast strange knowledge which he had gained from his speech and friendship with animals had brought him the power to do things that no other human being would dare to try."

FRIED BANANAS OR "PLATANOSFRITOS"

"And as it grew near to suppertime, the man asked us to sup with him. This of course we were very glad to do. And after the meal was over (very nice dishes they were, mostly cooked in olive oil – I particularly liked the <u>fried bananas</u>) we sat outside on the pavement again and went on talking far into the night."

VOCABULARY WORD

PONDEROUS – adjective
of great weight, heavy, massive
"Well, let us hope that the <u>ponderous</u> fragment does not lose its equilibriosity, for I don't believe it would stop at the center of the earth. More likely, it would fall right through the world and come out the other side."

 Which adventure of Dr. Dolittle's did you like the best? Make up your own imaginary place where you and Dr. Dolittle could go together. What would it be like? You could draw a picture of your imaginary place.

From THE VOYAGES OF DR. DOLITTLE, by Hugh Lofting, permission by Penguin Random House

DEEP FRIED BANANA BITES
WITH HONEY

September 21st, International Banana Festival

INGREDIENTS

3 bananas
1 ¼ cup pancake mix
2 T. sugar
1 egg
½ tsp. vanilla
¼ cup powdered sugar
vegetable oil for frying
honey warmed in the
microwave

INSTRUCTIONS

- Fill a pan with oil ½ " deep and heat to 350-375 degrees.
- Line a plate with paper towels and set aside.
- Slice the bananas into ¾ " slices.
- Combine pancake mix, sugar, milk, egg, and vanilla.
- Dip each banana slice in batter and allow excess to drip off. I used a bamboo skewer for dipping.
- Place in oil and fry for 1 – 2 minutes on each side or until golden brown. I had a helper turning the bites and putting them on the paper towel, while I added more bananas to the pan.
- Place banana bites on a serving plate and drizzle with warm honey.
- Sprinkle with powdered sugar and eat while they are still warm.

Adapted from: www.cincyshopper.com/deep-fried-bananas-bites

A DAY ON SKATES

Newbery Honor 1935, By Hilda van Stockum

Reading Level Grades 3 - 6

It is a snowy winter in the village of Friesland and twin brothers Evert and Afke are delighted that their teacher is taking the whole class on an all-day ice skating adventure. Teacher doesn't know what he is getting into as a few of the boys find their way into some mischief.

MY FAVORITE QUOTE

"Nothing was there before him but a glittering ribbon of ice winding itself between snow-covered fields and inviting him to breathe deeply and to go on as fast as his legs would carry him."

GINGERBREAD

" 'I am giving you four currant buns each, two slices of <u>gingerbread</u>, and also some money for hot chocolate on the way,' said Mother."

VOCABULARY WORD

CONSTERNATION – noun
a feeling of anxiety or shock
"In the meantime, there was great <u>consternation</u> in the church. Teacher was surprised to find four of the boys missing."

? How do you think the boys felt after they got themselves locked in the church tower? In what ways are the boys and girls in the story the same as children today?

From A DAY ON SKATES, written and illustrated by Hilda van Stockum, copyright 1934 Harper and Brothers. 2007 Commemorative Edition by Bethlehem Books. Used by permission of Bethlehem Books.

SPICY GINGERBREAD

June 5th, National Gingerbread Day

Ingredients

2 ¼ C. flour	½ t. baking soda
½ t. salt	2 t. ground ginger
1 t. cinnamon	½ t. ground cloves
½ t. nutmeg ½ t. allspice 1 t. cocoa	
3 T. minced crystallized ginger	

½ C. melted, cooled butter
¾ C. mild molasses
¾ C. sugar
½ C. buttermilk
½ C. milk
1 large egg

- Heat oven to 350 degrees. Grease bottom and sides of 11x7 or 9x9 baking dish. Dust with flour.
- Whisk together flour, baking soda, salt, ground ginger, cinnamon, cloves, nutmeg, allspice, crystallized ginger, and cocoa in medium bowl.
- Beat butter, molasses, sugar, buttermilk, milk and egg in large bowl with electric mixer on low.
- Add dry ingredients and beat on medium speed until batter is smooth and thick, about 1 minute, scraping down the sides of the bowl as needed. Do not overmix. Pour the batter into the prepared pan and smooth the surface.
- Bake until the top springs back when lightly touched and the edges have pulled away from the pan sides, about 40 minutes. Cool on wire rack for at least 10 minutes.
- Serve warm or at room temperature. Can be wrapped in plastic, then foil, and refrigerated up to 5 days.

Reprinted with permission from Cook's Illustrated magazine. For more information about this magazine or other publications by American Test Kitchen call 800-526-8442. Selected articles and recipes, as well as subscription information, are also available online at www.cooksillustrated.com

ON THE BANKS OF PLUM CREEK

Newbery Honor 1937, By Laura Ingalls Wilder

Reading Level Grades 4 - 7

ON THE BANKS OF PLUM CREEK
is the 4th of Laura Ingalls books based on her childhood. The Ingalls have left their little house on the Kansas prairie by covered wagon. They have settled on the banks of Plum Creek in Minnesota. Mary and Laura go to school for the first time. The Ingalls family work together to overcome obstacles of natural disasters, such as devastating grasshoppers, fire and prairie blizzards.

MY FAVORITE QUOTE

"Pa said, 'No pesky mess of grasshoppers can beat us! We'll do something! You'll see! We'll get along somehow. We're healthy, we've got a roof over our heads; we're better off than lots of folks. I'll find something to do. Don't you worry!' "

RUBY LOUISE FRANKLIN DALTON'S CORN BREAD

"Ma went gently between the table and the stove. In the middle of the table she set a milk-pan full of beautiful brown baked beans, and now from the oven she took the square baking pan full of golden corn bread. The rich brown smell and the sweet golden smell curled deliciously together in the air.

VOCABULARY WORD

CONTRADICTED – verb
to say the opposite of what someone else has said
"Laura looked up the glistening prickly golden haystack. She had to be high up in that blue sky. 'Laura!' Mary cried. 'Pa said we mustn't!' 'He did not, either!' she contradicted."

Ma and Pa do not agree about whether they should move west. Ma is worried about not having schools or communities, but Pa thinks the west is a land of opportunity. If it were you, would you have wanted to stay or go west?

RUBY LOUISE FRANKLIN DALTON'S CORN BREAD

January 22, National Southern Food Day

INGREDIENTS

1 C. flour
1 C. corn meal
3 T. sugar
½ t. baking powder
½ t. baking soda
1 t. salt
2/3 C. buttermilk
1 egg
¼ C. melted butter

INSTRUCTIONS

- Mix together the flour, corn meal, sugar, baking powder, baking soda, and salt.
- Mix together buttermilk and egg, and add all at once to dry ingredients.
- Stir in shortening or butter.
- Bake at 400 degrees.
- Put in preheated muffin pans or skillet (sprayed with cooking oil).
- Bake about 25 minutes.   Thanks mom. I love this recipe.

6

PANCAKES-PARIS

Newbery Honor 1948, By Claire Huchet Bishop

Reading Level Grades 3 - 5

This story of generosity takes place in Paris after the end of WWII. Two American soldiers befriend Charles and give him a box of pancake mix. Charles' quest is to figure out how to make crepes from the mix for Mardi Gras. He doesn't know how to read the English directions on the box, but he solves the problem and surprises his mom and sister.

MY FAVORITE QUOTE

"The room was warm from the cooking and the people in it. And though there was only the kerosene lamp, it was bright and cheerful, and they were all laughing because it was all so good."

CREPES

" 'It's a stuff made with flour,' said Charles. 'And e-g-g, and m-i-l-k,' said Louise. 'And you fry it in a frying pan, all flat and thin,' said Remi."

VOCABULARY WORD

BASKING – verb
to lie or be exposed to a pleasant warmth
"Charles and Zezette told her about the nice basking in the sun after school, and Mother was happy and she said, 'It's well. It will do you good.'"

? What did Charles do to solve his problem of how to make crepes from the pancake mix the American soldier had given him? Why do you think the American soldiers wanted to surprise Charles and his family?

DESSERT OR BREAKFAST CREPES

January 2nd is The Day of Crepes in France

INGREDIENTS

2 cups flour
4 eggs
1 c. of milk
1 c. of water
pinch of salt
4 T melted butter
5 T sugar
2 tsp. vanilla extract
3 tsp. almond extract
½ tsp. nutmeg

INSTRUCTIONS

- In a blender, add the milk, water, eggs, extracts, nutmeg, flour, sugar, salt, and melted butter. Blend for about 30 seconds until smooth. Scrape sides.
- Preheat oiled pan to medium high.
- Pour ¼ cup of batter in the pan and whirl the pan to thin the batter.
- Cook until the crepe is covered with bubbles and the bottom is light brown.
- Flip it over and allow the other side to cook for about 1 minute.
- Serve your crepes hot with your favorite fillings.

We love our crepes with raspberries, huckleberries, whipped cream, or chocolate spread.

Recipe by: Melissa Dalton Hunt

THE 21 BALLOONS

Newbery Medal 1948, By William Pene du Bois

Reading Level Grades 4 - 7

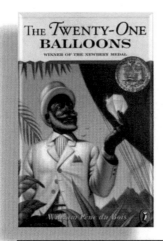

Professor William Sherman, a retired teacher, is ready for an adventure of drifting around the world alone in his hot air balloon. He intends to fly across the Pacific Ocean. Instead, he lands on Krakatoa, an island full of inventions and great wealth. Three weeks later he is rescued in the ocean not with one balloon, but twenty balloons and ready to tell of his adventure. The events and ideas of the story are based on Mr. du Bois' imagination and scientific facts.

MY FAVORITE QUOTE

"The gentle motion of the balloon and my soft inflated mattress made a combination for perfect sleeping. I spent the early evening on my porch in solitary contentment, studying the stars. I think I can honestly say that my few days flying over the Pacific in the Globe were the happiest days of my life."

SPAGHETTI

"There was a tremendous variety of cooking to be had... 'What a wonderful place this Island is,' I exclaimed. I am certainly looking forward to "I" Day (Italian Day) because I love spaghetti. 'Mr. I's Italian restaurant serves the best,' assured Mr. F."

VOCABULARY WORD

PINNACLE – noun
the pinnacle is the highest point
"There was a flagpole at this pinnacle from which waved the American Flag above."

 Why do you think the people in the book lived on the dormant volcano when, with a handful of diamonds, they could live a life of ease and comfort in another country? If you were going on a trip around the world, what would you take with you?

BAKED ZUCCHINI ANGEL HAIR

INGREDIENTS

1 lb. lean ground beef
8 oz. uncooked spaghetti or angel hair pasta
1 large bottle (26.5) spaghetti sauce with chunky vegetables
2 chopped medium sized red peppers
2 sliced medium sized zucchini
¼ cup chopped onions
1 cup grated cheddar cheese
1 cup grated mozzarella cheese
½ cup grated Parmesan cheese
1 small can sliced olives
salt, pepper, Italian seasoning

January 4th, National Spaghetti Day

INSTRUCTIONS

- Cook the spaghetti or angel hair according to the package directions. Cook to al dente, drain, and set aside.
- Meanwhile brown the ground beef, drain, and return it to the skillet. Add spaghetti sauce, salt, pepper, and Italian seasoning to taste.
- In another skillet saute the peppers, zucchini, and onions in olive oil until just starting to wilt.
- Using a 12 x 8 inch baking dish (or something close) assemble in the following order: layer of spaghetti sauce, cooked pasta, cheddar cheese, sauted veggies, pasta, spaghetti sauce, mozzarella cheese, sauted veggies, parmesan cheese, and top with olives.
- Bake at 350 degrees for 25 minutes.   Recipe by: Melissa Dalton Hunt

THE WHEEL ON THE SCHOOL

Newbery Medal 1955, By Meindert DeJong

Reading Level Grades 4 - 7

"Why do the storks no longer come to the little Dutch village of Shora to nest?" Lina asked her teacher which lead the whole class to an investigation. Six students engage practically the whole population of Shora in an effort to attract storks to nest on the town's roofs again. Not only do the people of Shora get their storks back, but they also discover what can happen when a community works together.

MY FAVORITE QUOTE

"But there's where things have to start – with a dream. Of course, if you just go on dreaming. Then it stays a dream and becomes stale and dead. But first to dream and then to do – isn't that the way to make a dream come true?"

OLIEBOLLEN (FAT BALLS)

"It was a picnic- steaming coffee and cakes and <u>fat balls</u>. That was what made it really a picnic and feast. You had hot chocolate milk only on the Queen's Birthday and <u>fat balls</u> only on Santa Claus Day. But now fat balls and chocolate all the same day!"

VOCABULARY WORD

TRIUMPHANTLY - adverb, something done in a victorious or proud manner. "He swung the wheel up over his head, held it there <u>triumphantly</u>, and stared up at it."

 How did the children get their community involved to help them achieve their goal? Have you ever excelled at something you thought you couldn't do?

OLIEBOLLEN – DUTCH DONUT
DEC. 31st (OIL BALLS) SPECIAL DUTCH NEW YEAR'S EVE TREAT

INGREDIENTS

1 ½ T. sugar
½ envelope dry yeast
½ cup warm milk
1 egg
½ t. almond extract
½ t. cinnamon
½ t. nutmeg
1 t. salt
2 C. flour
Lemon zest from ½ of small lemon
½ of a Granny Smith apple, peeled,
cored and diced
3 C. oil for frying
¼ C. sugar + 1 T. cinnamon mixed
together in a brown paper bag
Makes about 1 ½ dozen

INSTRUCTIONS

- In your mixer, pour ¼ C. of the warm milk. Then add the sugar and yeast, mixing at low speed. Let it rest for 5 minutes.
- Add other ¼ C. of the milk, egg, almond extract, cinnamon, nutmeg, and salt.
- Add the flour a cup at a time and mix it on high for two minutes.
- The mixture should become a solid ball. Add water a little bit at a time if too dry.
- If it is too much like cake batter, add flour a little bit at a time.
- Mix in the lemon zest and the diced apple.
- Place in a greased bowl, turning to coat the dough. Cover it, and let it rise in a warm place until it has doubled in size for about 1 hour.
- Punch down the dough lightly and form into small balls about 1 ½ inches in diameter.
- Let the balls rise for 20 minutes in a warm place.
- Heat 2 inches of oil in a skillet. Fry the balls for about 3 minutes, about 5 at a time, turning until they are golden brown all over.
- Set them on paper towels. Then put each batch in the bag to shake and coat with the cinnamon and sugar.

Inspired by www.fabulousfoods.com

12

MIRACLES ON MAPLE HILL

Newbery Medal 1957, By Virginia Sorensen

Reading Level Grades 3 – 6

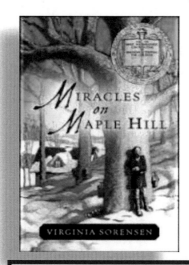

Marly's family moves to the country so that her father, a prisoner-of-war suffering from post-traumatic stress disorder, can learn to function once more. The family helps their neighbors, Mr. and Mrs. Chris, with their maple syrup business. When Mr. Chris becomes ill, Marly's family steps up to help make the syrup. Marly's father's condition improves and the family bonds more closely.

MY FAVORITE QUOTE

"It's the beginning, Marly thought. Just as Mr. Chris had said, the syrup is spring. It's the heart and blood of the maple trees; it has the gold of the leaves in it and the brown of the bark. It's the sun shining. It's snow melting. It's the bright new air and the earth as it starts pushing – pushing -pushing."

MAPLE SYRUP

"Mr. Chris said he had to boil away forty gallons of sap to make one little gallon of <u>syrup</u>."

VOCABULARY WORD

SPILE – noun
spout for conducting sap from the tree "The sap was coming so fast that before they got the buckets on, the <u>spiles</u> were dripping."

What does this story teach you about working together? What changes did the family see in their dad when they were at Maple Hill? How did the relationships in the family change?

HOMEMADE MAPLE SYRUP

December 17th, National Maple Syrup Day

INGREDIENTS

1 C. boiling water
1 C. granulated sugar
1 C. brown sugar
1 T. butter
2 t. molasses
2 t. maple extract or Mapleine
(imitation maple flavor)
1 t. vanilla extract
½ t. hazelnut extract

Makes about 2 cups

INSTRUCTIONS:

- Boil the water in a medium sized pot.
- Add the sugars and stir until dissolved over medium heat.
- Add the butter and molasses and simmer for 5 minutes.
- Add the extracts and simmer until the syrup thickens.
- Cool and put in dispenser. Store in refrigerator.

Recipe by: Melissa Dalton Hunt

THE CRICKET IN TIMES SQUARE

Newbery Honor 1961, By George Selden

Reading Level Grades 3 - 6

This story is about Chester, a musical cricket from Connecticut who finds himself transported to Times Square in New York City. He is found by a boy named Mario who keeps him as a pet. Chester reveals his musical chirping talent and becomes famous. Mario senses that Chester has become unhappy and has to decide what he wants to do with his life.

MY FAVORITE QUOTE

"Eyes that looked worried grew soft and peaceful, tongues left off chattering, and ears full of the city's rustling were rested by the cricket's melody."

CHOW MEIN

Sai Fong served fried rice and <u>chow mein</u> with cashew nuts to Chester and Mario.

VOCABULARY WORD

EAVESDROPPING – verb
listening secretly to a private conversation of others
Tucker Mouse definitely enjoyed <u>eavesdropping</u> on human beings.

 Why does Chester "sing" for the first time? How does his singing affect others? Why does Chester decide to retire?

CHOW MEIN

February 6th, National Chopsticks Day

INGREDIENTS

¼ C. light salt soy sauce
1 T. brown sugar
1 t. dried minced garlic
¼ t. ground ginger
1/8 t. black pepper
3 T. vegetable oil
2- 6 oz. pkgs. Chow mein noodles
2/3 C. diagonally chopped celery
1 medium sized onion, thinly sliced
2 C. chopped cabbage
¼ Cup shredded carrots
¼ C. chopped water chestnuts

INSTRUCTIONS

- In a small bowl combine soy sauce, brown sugar, garlic, ginger, and black pepper. Set aside.
- Cook the noodles as directed on package. Rinse noodles well, drain, and set aside.
- Heat oil in a large wok or skillet. Add celery and onion and saute for about 1 – 2 minutes or until onions start to become soft and transparent. Add cabbage and saute an additional minute or so. Add the water chestnuts and carrots if desired.
- Toss the noodles and soy sauce mixture with the vegetables over medium-high heat for an additional 2 – 3 minutes or until noodles are heated through.

Permission and Adaptation from Favorite Family Recipes
www.favfamilyrecipes.com

A WRINKLE IN TIME

Newbery Medal 1963, By Madeleine L'Engle

Reading Level Grades 5 – 8

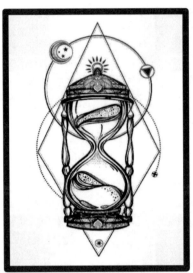

A Wrinkle in Time is a science fantasy novel of the adventures in space and time of the Murry family. Their father, who has mysteriously disappeared, was working on a project called a tesseract; experimenting with fifth dimension time travel for the government. Now the time has come for Meg, her friend Calvin, and Charles Wallace to rescue him. But can they outwit the forces of evil they will encounter on their journey through space?

MY FAVORITE QUOTE

"I don't understand it any more than you do, but one thing I've learned is that you don't have to understand things for them to BE."

COCOA

Meg finally relaxed being in the warm, light kitchen with the smell of <u>cocoa</u> on the stove.

VOCABULARY WORD

PRODIGIOUS – adjective
something big, powerful, or extraordinary
Charles Wallace's word of the day was "exclusive". His mother said that was a <u>prodigious</u> word.

Where and why do Calvin, Charles Wallace, and Meg go with Mrs. Whatsit, Mrs. Who, and Mrs. Which? The people on the planet Camazotz have no crime, no responsibility, and no decisions to make. What do you think of their society?

DARK AND STORMY NIGHT HOT CHOCOLATE

December 12th, National Cocoa Day

INGREDIENTS

1 (14 oz.) can sweetened
condensed milk
½ c. unsweetened Dutch
Cocoa
1 ½ t. vanilla extract
1 t. almond extract
½ t. nutmeg
1/8 t. salt
5 ½ C. water
¼ heavy cream

Serves 8

INSTRUCTIONS:

- In a large saucepan combine sweetened condensed milk, cocoa, vanilla and almond extracts, nutmeg and salt.
- Mix well over medium heat.
- Slowly stir in hot water and heavy cream.
- Continue stirring occasionally, but do not boil.
- Top with whipped cream and a pinch of nutmeg on top.

You probably won't have any of this yummy hot chocolate left, but if you do, store it covered in the refrigerator.

Recipe by: Melissa Dalton Hunt

18

FROG AND TOAD TOGETHER

Newbery Honor 1973, By Arnold Lobe

Reading Level Grades Preschool – Grade 3

"Frog and Toad Together" is a collection of stories about two best friends, Frog and Toad, of course. The stories feature flowers, cookies, bravery, dreams, and, most of all, friendship. My favorite story, "Cookies," takes place at Frog's house when Toad brings cookies to share. They are so good they can't stop eating them! In the end there is a lesson learned about will power.

MY FAVORITE QUOTE

" 'Frog, I am glad to have a brave friend like you,' said Toad. 'And I am happy to know a brave person like you, Toad.' They stayed in the closet for a long time, just feeling very brave together."

COOKIES

" 'We must stop eating!' cried Toad as he ate another.' 'Yes,' said Frog, reaching for a <u>cookie</u>, 'we need will power.' 'What is will power?' asked Toad. 'Will power is trying hard <u>not</u> to do something that you really want to do,' said Frog."

VOCABULARY WORD

THEATER – noun
a building where plays are performed or movies are shown
" 'Frog, can you be as wonderful as this?' said Toad as he danced all over the stage. There was no answer. Toad looked out into the <u>theater</u>. Frog was so small that he could not be seen or heard. 'Frog, what have I done?' cried Toad."

 Does doing something dangerous show you are brave? Is there a food you love so much that it is really hard to stop yourself from eating it?

MIMMIE'S CHOCOLATE CHIP COOKIES

My grand kids' favorite cookies.

This makes a nice, big batch.

May 15th, National Chocolate Chip Cookies Day

INGREDIENTS

2 C. oil
2 t. soda
3 C. brown sugar
4 eggs
1 t. vanilla extract
½ t. almond extract
1 t. salt
5 C. flour
2 – 3 C. chocolate chips

INSTRUCTIONS

- Beat the oil, soda, brown sugar, and eggs until foamy.
- Add the vanilla and almond extracts.
- Add the flour and salt, one cup at a time.
- Add the chocolate chips. Dough will be very stiff.
- Chill the dough before baking.
- Bake at 350 degrees for 10-12 minutes using parchment paper.

Recipe by: Melissa Dalton Hunt

ABEL'S ISLAND

Newbery Honor 1977, By William Steig

Reading Level Grades 3 - 5

Abel, a mouse, and his wife Amanda are enjoying a picnic when they are interrupted by a fierce rainstorm. Amanda's scarf is blown away by a gust of wind, and Abel gallantly sets off to retrieve it. The storm washes Abel into a river and he is deposited on an island, stranded through the winter. Abel lives through some hard times, but he learns that he is smarter and braver than he thought he was.

MY FAVORITE QUOTE

"The conviction grew in him that the earth and the sky knew he was there and also felt friendly, so he was not really alone."

FAMILY PICNIC

Abel and Amanda's delightful picnic consisted of small sandwiches of pot cheese and watercress, along with hard-boiled quail egg, onion, and olives.

VOCABULARY WORD

MAROONED – verb

to be placed somewhere that is difficult or impossible to get away from
Abel realized that he was <u>marooned</u> on an island and there was no one to help him but himself.

? Abel is a mouse who has never worked. What things did he discover he could do to survive being marooned on the island? How was Abel a better Abel after surviving his year on the island? How does working through a difficult situation change you?

ABEL'S ISLAND PICNIC

April 23rd, National Picnic Day

At the beginning of "Abel's Island", Abel and his wife, Amanda, are enjoying a late- summer picnic date. You can create your own family picnic with similar types of food.

My spring picnic date with my husband included mini bagels with cream cheese (pot cheese), arugula baby spinach (instead of watercress), red onions, cottage cheese, hard boiled eggs, (instead of quail eggs), and black olives. And…our favorite bubbly drink, sparkling cider in fancy glasses. Ooooh-la-la!

SARAH PLAIN AND TALL

Newbery Medal 1986, By Patricia MacLachlan

Reading Level Grades 3 - 6

Anna and Caleb's lives are changed forever when their widowed papa advertises for a mail-order bride. Sarah, from Maine, comes by train and agrees to stay for a month. Sarah brings Seal, her cat, gifts from the sea, and singing and laughter to the Witting home. Anna and Caleb are captivated by Sarah and hope she stays.

STEW AND BAKED BREAD

"We ate Sarah's <u>stew</u>, the light coming through the windows. Papa had baked bread that was still warm from the fire."

VOCABULARY WORD

EERIE – adjective
something that is mysterious and creepy
"Papa closed the door, shutting out some of the sounds of the storm. The barn was <u>eerie</u> and half lighted, like dusk without a lantern."

MY FAVORITE QUOTE

"I will always miss my old home, but the truth of it is, I would miss you more."

 Why would Sarah come so far away from Maine to find someone to marry? Of all the nice things that Sarah does for her family, what do you think is the kindest?

SARAH'S BEEF STEW

Dec. 13th, National Beef Stew Day

Ingredients

1 ½ lbs. stew meat
2 T. olive oil
4 T. flour
salt and pepper
1 pkg. beef stew seasoning mix
1 pkg. beefy onion soup mix
2 t. Worcestershire sauce
1 T. brown sugar
½ t. rosemary
½ t. thyme
5 C. frozen stew vegetables
5 C. of water

Serves 6

INSTRUCTIONS

- While the olive oil is heating in a frying pan, coat the stew meat in flour, salt and pepper, and brown on all sides. Transfer the meat into a large pot.
- Add the seasoning mix and onion soup mix, Worcestershire sauce, brown sugar, rosemary, and thyme.
- Add the frozen stew vegetables.
- Add the water and bring to a boil.
- Simmer until stew thickens and the vegetables are tender.

Bake some "Ruby Louise's Corn Bread" to add to
"Sarah's Stew" for a delicious meal.

Recipe by: Melissa Dalton Hunt

MANIAC MAGEE

Newbery Medal 1991, By Jerry Spinelli

Reading Level Grades 5 – 8

Jeffrey Magee is orphaned at the age of three. After living with his unhappy aunt and uncle for eight years, he decides to run, and he really runs. In the town of Two Mills he becomes a local legend for feats of athleticism and he changes the lives of a racially divided small town.

MY FAVORITE QUOTE

"Maniac loved his new life. He loved the early morning when it seemed as if the whole world had been created just before he woke up. He loved the silence and the solitude. He loved the sound of pancake batter hissing on the griddle."

MARS BARS

"The kid, as you probably guessed by now, was none other than Mars Bar Thompson. Then suddenly he was smiling. He held up the candy bar, an inch from Maniac's lips. 'Wanna bite?' "

VOCABULARY WORD

PANDEMONIUM – noun
a wild uproar or disorder; chaos
"This time the ball cleared the fence on the fly. Three more pitches. Three more home runs. Pandemonium on the sidelines."

 What makes Maniac a legend? At the end of the story, Maniac finally gets a home. Explain how that happens.

HOMEMADE MARS BARS

December 28th, Chocolate Candy Day

INGREDIENTS

Parchment paper
<u>Bottom Chocolate Layer</u>: 14 oz. chocolate almond bark
<u>Nougat Layer</u>: 5 T butter, 1 ½ C. granulated sugar, ½ C. light brown sugar, 1/3 C. evaporated milk, 2 7 oz. bottles of marshmallow crème, 1 C. chocolate spread
<u>Caramel Layer</u>: 1 14 oz. pkg. caramel candies ¼ C. heavy cream, ½ T. butter
<u>Top Chocolate Layer and Sides of Bars</u>: 20 oz. chocolate almond bark-use what you need.

INSTRUCTIONS

- Line the bottom and sides of a greased 9' x 13" baking pan with parchment paper.
- To make the bottom chocolate layer, melt the 14 oz. almond bark in the microwave until smooth. Spread the chocolate into the baking pan and refrigerate until set, about 15 minutes.
- To make the nougat layer, melt the butter over medium heat in a pan; add white and brown sugars and evaporated milk. Bring to a boil and cook 5 minutes while stirring.
- Remove from the heat and add marshmallow crème and chocolate spread. Pour over the bottom layer and gently spread mixture. Return to refrigerator for 20 – 30 minutes.
- To make the caramel layer, place the unwrapped caramel candy, butter, and cream in a medium saucepan. Place over low heat and stir until the mixture has completely melted and is smooth. Pour in the pan and quickly spread over the nougat layer. Return to refrigerator for 20 – 30 minutes.
- To make the top chocolate layer and sides, melt the 20 oz. of almond bark (as needed if you want so that it doesn't harden).
- Remove the candy pan from the refrigerator and peel off the parchment paper. Use a large piece of parchment paper for your work place. Working with 1 inch rows at a time cut into 1 inch squares, keeping the remainder of the candy in the freezer until needed. Coat the tops and sides of the bars with the chocolate almond bark. Store in a sealed container in the refrigerator.

Adapted from recipe: Candy Man's Billion Dollar Candy Bar by Libby Murphy
www.twirlandtaste.com/2012/12/take-bite-of-candy-mans-billion-dollar.html

HOLES

Newbery Medal 1999, By Louis Sachar

Reading Level Grades 5 – 8

Stanley Yelnats is unjustly sent to a boys' correctional camp. The boys there "build character" by spending all day digging holes. Stanley realizes the boys are digging because the warden is looking for something, and Stanley digs up a new sense of himself.

MY FAVORITE QUOTE

"Nothing in life is easy. But that's no reason to give up. You'll be surprised what you can accomplish if you set your mind to it."

SPICED PEACHES

No one could make <u>spiced peaches</u> better than Miss Katherine Barlow.

VOCABULARY WORD

PRECIPICE – noun
a cliff with a vertical face
With every step Stanley took the huge <u>precipice</u> grew in front of him.

After digging his first hole, Stanley feels proud. Why do you think he feels that way? When Stanley carries Zero up the mountain he focused on one step at a time. How do you tackle a job that seems too big for you?

SPICED PEACHES

August 22, Eat a Peach Day

INGREDIENTS

2 large cans peach halves
(drain and save the syrup in a
separate bowl)
1 c. honey
½ c. light brown sugar
½ c. cider vinegar
¼ t. salt
¼ t. nutmeg
3 cinnamon sticks
¼ t. ground ginger
1t. whole cloves

INSTRUCTIONS

- In a saucepan, simmer the following ingredients for 10 minutes:
  1 cup of peach syrup, honey, light brown sugar, apple cider, salt, nutmeg, cinnamon sticks, ground ginger, and whole cloves.

- Place the peaches in a serving dish and pour the spiced syrup over the peaches. Let it cool. Then cover and chill in the refrigerator for 24 hours.

Recipe By: Melissa Dalton Hunt

BUD, NOT BUDDY

Newbery Medal 2000, By Christopher Paul Curtis

Reading Level Grade 4 - 7

BUD, NOT BUDDY is the story of a 10-year-old orphan, Bud Caldwell, during the Great Depression. After Bud has lived in several foster homes, he runs away in search of his father in Grand Rapids. The only thing he takes with him is his suitcase filled with his own important things and a clue to who his father might.

MY FAVORITE QUOTE

"A bud is a flower-to-be. A flower-in-waiting. Waiting for just the right warmth and care to open up. It's the little fist of love waiting to unfold and be seen by the world. And that's you."

SWEET POTATO PIE

"It was the best meal I'd ever had, and when it was done Miss Tyla brought me a dessert she called 'On the House'. It was a piece of warm sweet potato pie with some white fluffy stuff called whipped cream swopped all over the top of it."

VOCABULARY WORD

SUSPICION – noun
suspecting something to be likely
"In the middle of the flyer was a blurry picture of the man I have a real good suspicion about. I've never met him, but I have a pretty good feeling that this guy must be my father."

 Bud realizes that he and Mr. Calloway share a collection. What do they collect and for whom? What relationship do they reveal? What new doors were open to Bud?

FESTIVE SWEET POTATO PIE

February 22nd, Cook a Sweet Potato Day

INGREDIENTS

3 C. cooked mashed sweet potatoes
½ C. sugar
½ C. sweetened condensed milk
½ C. heavy whipping cream
¼ C. melted butter
2 beaten eggs plus 1 egg yolk
1 t. Vanilla, ½ t. nutmeg
½ t. cinnamon

Topping Ingredients
1 C. coconut
1 C. brown sugar packed
1/3 C. flour, 1/3 C. melted butter
1 C. chopped pecans

INSTRUCTIONS

- Preheat oven to 350 degrees.
- Combine first 9 ingredients, mixing well. Spoon into deep dish BEST PIE CRUST, recipe below.
- Combine topping ingredients and sprinkle over the top of the sweet potatoes.
- Bake for 55-60 minutes or until a knife inserted in the center comes out clean.

BEST PIE CRUST

Ingredients: 1 egg, ¼ C. of water, 1 T vinegar, 2 ½ C. flour,
1 t. salt, 1 C. of shortening

- Beat the egg with the water and vinegar
- Mix the dry ingredients together.
- Add the shortening and mix, cutting to the size of peas.
- Add the liquid a little at a time, mixing well. Form into two balls.

The pie filling is modified from my mother's recipe, Ruby Louise Franklin Dalton's FESTIVE SWEET POTATO CASSEROLE. The pie crust I named BEST PIE CRUST is a recipe from my mother-in-law, Betty Patterson Hunt.

BECAUSE OF WINN-DIXIE

Newbery Honor 2001, By Kate DiCamillo

Reading Level Grades 3 - 6

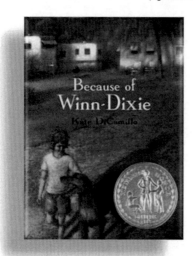

Opal finds it is hard to make friends when she moves to a new town. But when she adopts a stray dog, it is just what she needs. Through the guidance of her very lovable Winn-Dixie, Opal learns lessons about reaching out. She finds friendship and forgiveness in the most unlikely people and places.

MY FAVORITE QUOTE

"You find the most important thing on your own. But in the meantime, you got to remember, you can't always judge people by the things they done. You got to judge them by what they are doing now."

MACARONI AND CHEESE

"My name is India Opal Buloni, and last summer my daddy, the preacher, sent me to the store for a box of macaroni-and-cheese, some white rice, and two tomatoes and I came back with a dog."

VOCABULARY WORD

MELANCHOLY – noun
a gloomy state of mind
"I got up out of bed and unwrapped a Littmus Lozenge and sucked on it hard and thought about my mama leaving me. That was a melancholy feeling."

 Why did Opal want to ask her dad ten things about her mother?
How did Winn-Dixie bring comfort and joy to the characters in this story?

SQUIGGLY EASY CHEESEY MAC

July 7th, National Macaroni Day

INGREDIENTS

1 (16) oz. Radiatore macaroni
½ cup butter
½ cup flour
1 tsp. salt   1 tsp. pepper
2 cups milk
2 ½ cups heavy cream
2 C. shredded sharp cheddar cheese
2 C. shredded Mozzarella cheese

TOPPING
25 Ritz crackers, crushed
3 T. melted butter

INSTRUCTIONS

- Add the Radiatore noodles to boiling water in a large pot. Drain the noodles and put them back in the large pot.
- Melt the butter in a medium sized pot.
- Whisk in the flour, salt, and pepper.
- Cook and stir over medium heat until bubbly.
- With low heat, add the shredded cheeses and stir until it is melted.
- Add the pasta to the cheese mixture.
- Put the cheesy pasta in a 9 x 13 inch pan.
  For the topping: Mix together the crushed Ritz crackers and the melted butter until crumbs are moist. Sprinkle over the top of the cheesy Radiatore. Bake about 20 minutes at 375 degrees until golden brown. You may have some cheesy sauce left over.

Adapted from: www.pumkinnspice.com/2015/01/26 creamy-stovetop-macaroni-cheese

A YEAR DOWN YONDER

Newbery Medal 2001, By Richard Peck

Reading Level Grades 6 - 8

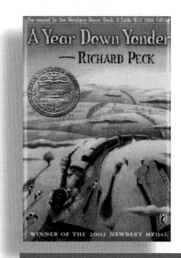

During the recession of 1937, Mary Alice is sent to live with her larger-than-life Grandma Dowdel. She is fifteen and faces a whole long year with her feisty grandma who likes to shake up the neighborhood. She discovers she better not predict how life with Grandma might be and gains a better understanding of this fearsome woman. A YEAR DOWN YONDER is a sequel to Richard Peck's A LONG WAY FROM CHICAGO.

MY FAVORITE QUOTE

"But what I remember best about that evening is the three of us walking home from church. I see us yet, strolling the occasional sidewalks with our arms around Grandma, just to keep her from skidding. And every star above us was a Christmas star."

BAKED APPLES WITH BROWN SUGAR

"Before evening was over, we of the younger set, except for Augie, bobbed for apples. I brought home a couple, and Granma and I baked them with brown sugar."

VOCABULARY WORD

MEANDERING – verb
"I was cold right through. We worked back to the road by a meandering route, leaving our own tracks behinds."

 How does Mary Alice's view of grandma change during the year that she lived with her? What does Mary Alice mean when she says, "Grandma has eyes in the back of her heart?"

BAKED APPLE SUNDAES

October, National Apple Month

INGREDIENTS

4 Honeycrisp apples
4 T. butter
1/3 C. brown sugar
1 t. cinnamon
½ t. nutmeg
ice cream
finely chopped peanuts
maraschino cherries

Caramel or chocolate ice cream topping

INSTRUCTIONS

- Preheat oven to 375 degrees.
- Prepare the apples: Cut off the top ¼ of the apple and core, being careful not to push through the bottom of the apple. With a kabob stick poke holes down in the top of the apples.
- In a saucepan, melt the butter, add the brown sugar and spices and stir until it simmers.
- Fill the core of the apple with caramel topping and cover the tops of the apples with the brown sugar topping.
- Bake in the oven for 25 – 30 minutes, checking to see if the apples are soft.
- Let apples cool; then top with ice cream, caramel, or chocolate topping, peanuts, and a cherry on the top.

Recipe by: Melissa Dalton Hunt

EVERYTHING ON A WAFFLE

Newberry Honor 2002, By Polly Horvath

Reading Level Grades 4-7

Primrose Squarp's parents disappeared in a typhoon, but Primrose refuses to believe they are dead. She lives in a small Canadian fishing village and loves to spend time at The Girl on the Red Swing restaurant where everything comes on a waffle. The owner, Kate Bowzer, takes her under her wing and teaches her how to cook. Primrose never gives up hope of finding her parents.

MY FAVORITE QUOTE

"Because, the only really interesting thing about someone that makes you want to explore them further is their heart."

WAFFLES

At the Girl on the Red Swing restaurant they always served everything on a <u>waffle</u>.

VOCABULARY WORD

HYPOTHERMIA – adjective   when body temperature becomes abnormally low
When Primrose's father was helping his wife on board the dinghy she was so wet he was worried about hypothermia.

Do you think you are influenced by the place you live or by the people that live around you? Have you ever just known something deep in your heart like Primrose did?

CINNAMON ROLL WAFFLES
WITH CREAM CHEESE "SYRUP"

August 24th, National Waffle Day

INGREDIENTS

FOR THE CINNAMON
WAFFLES:
2 cans cinnamon rolls

FOR THE CREAM CHEESE
SYRUP:
1 C. powdered sugar
4 oz. cream cheese, softened
8 T. unsalted butter
1 t. pure vanilla extract

Yield: 16 Waffles

INSTRUCTIONS

FOR THE CINNAMON ROLL WAFFLES:
- Preheat waffle iron to medium-high.
- Spray your waffle iron with cooking spray or brush on oil.
- Place one cinnamon roll on each square and close iron.
- Bake until golden brown about 1 – 2 minutes.

FOR THE CREAM CHEESE SYRUP:
- Melt butter in saucepan over low heat.
- Stir softened cream cheese into butter and then whisk in powdered sugar and vanilla extract until smooth.
- Drizzle over cinnamon roll waffles.

Recipe with permission from Tara Kuczykowski, Founder Table for 7 Media, LLC
http://unsophisticooki.com/cinnamon-roll-waffles

THE TALE OF DESPEREAUX

Newbery Medal 2004, by Kate DiCamillo

Reading Level Grades 3-6

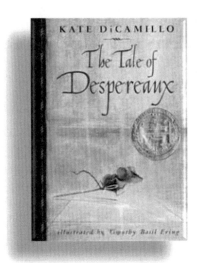

This is a heartwarming story of a brave little mouse named Despereaux, a lost rat, a slave girl, and a beautiful princess. When the little mouse with a big heart falls in love with Princess Pea, it sets in motion a chain of events that will require Despereaux to be as brave as the knights he reads about. Despereaux learns that everything cannot always be sweetness and light.

MY FAVORITE QUOTE

"Forgive, reader, is, I think, something very much like hope and love, a powerful, wonderful thing."

SOUP

"The Queen loved soup. She loved soup more than anything in the world except for the Princes Pea and the King. And because the queen loved it, soup was served in the castle for every banquet, every lunch, and every dinner. And what <u>soup</u> it was!"

VOCABULARY WORD

PERFIDY – noun   deliberate betrayal, untrustworthy
" '<u>Perfidy</u>' was certainly the word that was in Depereaux's mind as the mice finally approached the narrow, steep stairs that led to the black hole of the dungeon."

How did the following characters betray their families? : Despereaux's father? Despereaux's brother? Miggery's father?   How do the following characters show acts of kindness?: Gregory, the cook? Miggery? Despereaux?

CLAM CHOWDER

AND WHAT SOUP IT IS!

February 4th, National Homemade Soup Day

INGREDIENTS

3 cans 8 oz. minced clams
1 cup diced onion
2 cups diced potatoes
1 C. diced celery
1 ½ cups butter
¾ cup flour
1 qt. half and half
1 ½ t. salt
½ t. sugar
Pepper to taste
Serves 12

INSTRUCTIONS

- Pour clam juice over the vegetables. Add water to cover.
- Cook 20 minutes, then simmer until potatoes are tender.
- Melt the butter in a separate pan.
- Slowly add flour with whisk. Cook for three minutes.
- Add half and half. Stir until it thickens and pour into vegetables.
- Add sugar, salt, and pepper.
- Add clams last.

This clam chowder is the Hunts' traditional Christmas Eve dinner. Enjoy it in bread bowls and party instead of washing dishes.

Recipe by: Melissa Dalton Hunt

PRINCESS ACADEMY

Newbery Honor 2006, by Shannon Hale

Reading Level Grades 4 - 7

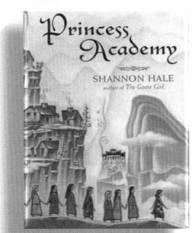

Miri lives with her people on Mt. Eskell. The lives of the young girls in the village change when it is announced that they are all to attend a Princess Academy that will prepare them to be royalty. At the end of the year, the prince will visit the academy and choose the girl who will be the next princess. When danger approaches, Miri is strong and faithful to her classmates and her village.

MY FAVORITE QUOTE

"She realized with sudden clarity that she did not want to live far away from the village. The mountain was home – the linder dust, the rhythm of the quarry, the people she knew as well as the feel of her own skin. And now, looking at them for perhaps the last time, she thought she loved them so much that her chest would burst.'

HONEYED NUTS

"Her mouth watered at the thought of hot sweet cakes, honeyed nuts for a holiday, and a bit saved to drizzle on biscuits some bleak winter evening."

VOCABULARY WORD

POTENTIAL – adjective   having the capacity to develop into something in the future   "As is the tradition, the king commanded an academy be created for the purpose of preparing the potential young ladies."

 Does Miri do the right thing by helping the other girls pass their princess exam, or is she cheating? How does learning to read affect Miri and the other girls around her?

HONEY ROASTED NUTS

October 22nd, National Nut Day

INGREDIENTS
1 C. nuts of your choice
¼ Cup + 1 T honey
1/8 t. Cinnamon
1/8th t. Cayenne pepper
¼ - ½ t. sea salt

INSTRUCTIONS

- Preheat oven to 350 degrees.
- Line a baking sheet with aluminum foil and set aside.
- In a small mixing bowl, combine honey, cinnamon, cayenne, and salt.
- Stir in the nuts until evenly coated.
- Pour the honey-coated nuts onto the baking sheet. Bake in the oven for 5 minutes or until golden brown.
- Let cool; then transfer to a serving bowl and enjoy.
  Nuts can be stored in an air-tight container for up to 3 days.

MOON OVER MANIFEST

Newbery Medal 2011, By Clare Vanderpool

Reading Level Grades 5 - 8

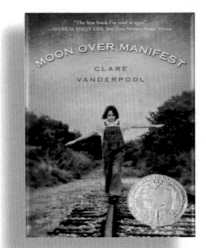

A young and adventurous girl named Abilene is sent to Manifest, Kansas, by her father in the summer of 1936. Abilene feels abandoned while her father works a railroad job. With only a few possessions Abilene jumps off the train in Manifest with a quest of learning about the boy her father once was.

MY FAVORITE QUOTE

" 'Seems like everyone in this town's got a story to tell,' Shady nodded. "I believe you're right about that. The Lord himself knew the power of a good story. How it can reach out and wrap around a person like a warm blanket.' "

ANGEL FOOD CAKE

"I was all ready to help parcel out the smidgeon of food when, lo and behold, Hattie Mae uncovered a huge angel food cake. It must have been twelve inches high. There was a new kind of hush as folks took their first bites and savored the sweet fluffiness of it."

VOCABULARY WORD

REMINISCE – verb
to recall past experiences, events
"How was I supposed to come up with a story for Sister Redempta or even a "Remember When...' to reminisce on with somebody else?"

How long does it take for Abilene to feel like the citizens of Manifest are like members of her family? Have you ever had to move and make new friends? How is Gideon's compass a symbol of hope to Abilene?

OVER THE MOON ANGEL FOOD CAKE

October 10th, National Angel Food Cake Day

INGREDIENTS

1 Cup Cake flour
¾ Cup powdered sugar
12 egg whites
1 ½ t. Cream of tartar
¼ tsp. salt
½ Cup sugar
1 ½ tsp. Vanilla extract
1 tsp. almond extract

INSTRUCTIONS

- Separate the eggs and allow them to stand at room temperature for 30 minutes.
- Preheat oven to 325 degrees. Lightly grease a 10 inch bundt pan with cooking spray.
- Mix together the Cake flour and powdered sugar in a bowl and set aside.
- Using your mixer whisk attachment, beat the egg whites, Cream of tartar, and salt until soft peaks form.
- Add the ½ Cup of sugar slowly, about 2 tablespoons at a time, to allow the sugar to dissolve. Whisk on high until stiff peaks form.
- Fold in the flour mixture using a spatula, one fourth at a time, then the extracts. Be careful not to overmix.
- Spoon into bundt pan. Gently cut through the batter with a thin metal spatula to eliminate air bubbles.
- Bake for 50 minutes until a golden brown. The cake is done when it springs back when lightly touched. Cool the cake in the pan on a wire rack. When cool, turn it upside down on a serving plate.

Inspired by a recipe: Best Ever Angel Food Cake by Amy Dong

Chew Out Loud http://www.chewoutloud.com

THE ONE AND ONLY IVAN

Newbery Medal 2013, By Katherine Applegate

Reading Level Grades 3 - 6

Ivan, a silverback gorilla, has lived in captivity at the Big Top Mall for 9,855 days. He rarely misses his life in the jungle. Mostly he thinks about his art. Along with Ivan, Stella the elephant and Bob, a stray dog, live at the mall. When baby elephant Ruby is brought to the Big Top Mall, things begin to change for the better.

MY FAVORITE QUOTE

"Humans speak too much. They chatter like chimps, crowding the world with their noise, even when they have nothing to say."

YOGURT RAISINS

"Humans do seem to enjoy watching me eat. Luckily I am always hungry. I am a gifted eater." "I don't want to leave the outside. It's a cloudless day and I've found just the right spot for a nap. But I relent when she adds yogurt raisins to the trail. She knows my weakness all too well.

VOCABULARY WORD

DOMAIN – noun
an area of owned territory
"My domain is made of thick glass and rusty metal and rough cement."

 What were the problems with keeping Ivan in the shopping mall?
What do you think about being able to buy a wild animal?

YOGURT AND WHITE CHOCOLATE COVERED RAISINS
(IVAN'S FAVORITE)

April 30th, National Raisin Day

INGREDIENTS

1 C. of nice fat raisins

1 small container of low fat Greek Yogurt

¼ cup of powdered sugar

1 – 12 oz. package of White Chocolate Melting Wafers

You will also need some waxed paper and some toothpicks.

INSTRUCTIONS

- Melt the white chocolate wafers in a small glass container according to the instructions on the package.
- Stir the container of Greek Yogurt.
- Mix the raisins and the powdered sugar in a small bowl.
- You will use the toothpicks to pick up the raisins one at a time.
- Next, dip the raisin in the yogurt, then dip it in the melted wafers.
- Use another toothpick to slide the raisin onto the waxed paper.
- After the raisins have hardened, dip them one more time in the melted wafers.

If you don't gobble them all up, you may store the rest in the refrigerator.

Recipe by: Melissa Dalton Hunt

FLORA AND ULYSSES

Newberry Medal 2014, By Kate DiCamillo

Reading Level Grades 3 - 6

Flora spends her time reading comic books and struggling to understand her parents' divorce. Then she is jolted into action when she rescues a squirrel who had been involved in an accident with a vacuum cleaner. She is astonished when the squirrel, Ulysses, demonstrates unbelievable powers of strength and flight after being revived. Flora is changed, too, as she discovers the possibility of hope and love in her heart.

MY FAVORITE QUOTE

"She loved his whiskers. She loved his happiness, his little head, his determined heart. She felt her heart seize up. She should have said those words to him."

DONUTS

"There were giant <u>donuts</u> with sprinkles, giant donuts powdered, iced! Giant donuts filled with things: jelly, cream, chocolate. He had never had a giant donut. How was a squirrel to choose?"

VOCABULARY WORD

CAPACIOUS – adjective
capable of holding much, spacious
"We will go and knock on the door of Mr. George Buckman. And he will open the door to us because he is <u>capacious</u> of heart."

 What makes Ulysses a superhero? Flora may not be a superhero, but she does some very heroic things. How does she help Ulysses? Her parents? William Spiver?

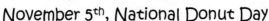

SPUDNUTS
November 5th, National Donut Day

A Teton Valley, Idaho / Wyoming recipe in honor of Vada Green

The best cook ever at the Alta, Wyoming Elementary School

INGREDIENTS

1 pint milk, scalded and cooled
4 ½ T. quick rising yeast, and 1 t.
sugar dissolved in cooled milk
4 T. butter
1 cup mashed potatoes
(I use instant potatoes)
3 T. sugar
2 beaten eggs
2 t. salt
5 – 6 cups of flour
<u>Glaze</u>
3 C. powdered sugar
6 – 8 T. warmed milk
2 – 3t. vanilla

INSTRUCTIONS

- Scald and cool 1 pint of milk.
- Add the quick rising yeast, and 1 t. sugar dissolved in cooled milk.
- Add the butter, mashed potatoes, 3 T. sugar, eggs, and salt.
- Mix all ingredients and add 5 – 6 cups of flour ½ cup at a time.
- I use my Kitchen Aid with dough hook for kneading. Once the flour is absorbed, mix for 8 – 10 minutes.
- Preheat oven to 170 degrees, then turn oven off. Lightly spray the dough with cooking spray, cover with a cloth, and set the bowl on your oven door to rise double in size. Punch down and rise again.
- Turn out dough onto a lightly floured surface. Use a generously floured rolling pin to roll dough to ½ inch thickness. Cut spudnuts. (I use a large size canning ring and then something smaller for cutting the hole.)
- Place on oven door again to rise until doubled in size.
- Fry in about 1 ½ inch oil at 375 degrees until lightly browned and drain on paper towels.
- Dip fried spudnuts into glaze and lay out on waxed paper until glaze is set.
  Now you will have enough spudnuts for you and your neighbors.

<u>Glaze</u>: Mix the glaze while your cut spudnuts are rising, then cover the glaze with plastic wrap. Sift the powdered sugar into a medium sized bowl. Slowly stir in the warm milk and vanilla extract. If the glaze isn't thin enough, stir in an additional T. of milk. Add chocolate or maple if desired.   46

28067355R00033

Made in the USA
Columbia, SC
14 October 2018